crows

crows

An Egg-to-Sky Story

Margaret Peot

muddy boots™

Essex, Connecticut

In the fall and winter, crows gather in large numbers. They are *roosting*. They do this for safety, to stay warm, to visit with other crows, or to find a mate.

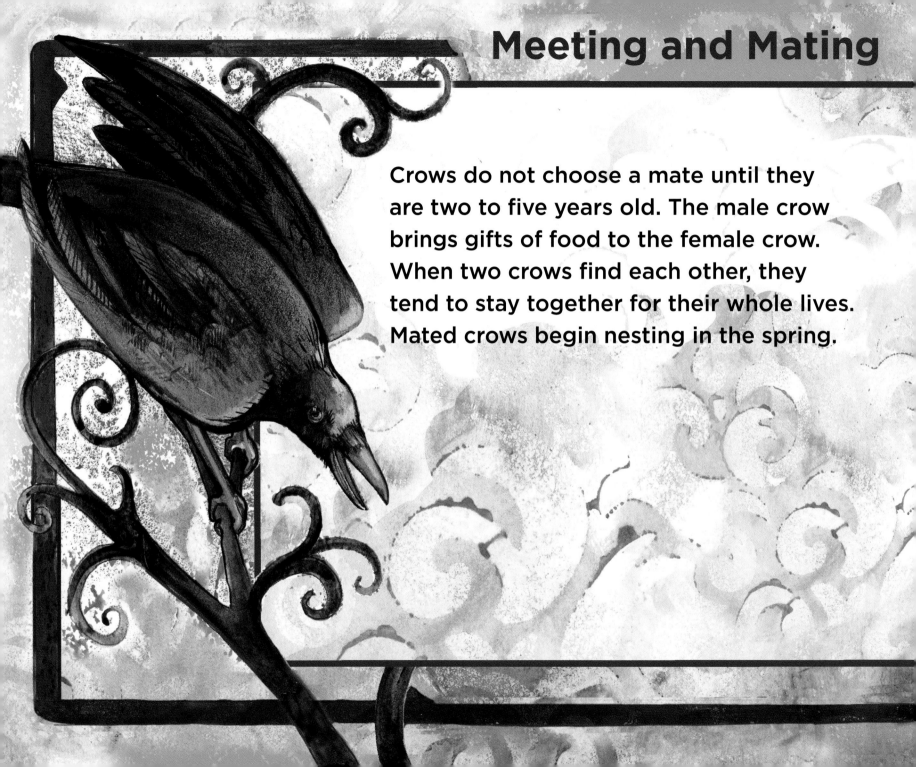

Meeting and Mating

Crows do not choose a mate until they are two to five years old. The male crow brings gifts of food to the female crow. When two crows find each other, they tend to stay together for their whole lives. Mated crows begin nesting in the spring.

Crows are quiet in the spring to hide their nest site. In a tall tree, where one or two branches meet the trunk of a tree in a V shape, the crow pair begins building together.

Building a Nest

The pair stuffs bigger branches into the V until they have a sturdy place to build a nest. They add smaller branches on top of big branches to make a bowl shape and then line the nest with soft grasses, moss, or fine bark strips.

Laying Eggs

In the soft center of the nest, the female crow lays three to seven greenish eggs with black and brown speckles. The eggs are about one and a half inches long. She usually lays one egg a day, in the morning.

Warming Them Day and Night

The female crow sits on the eggs to warm them until they hatch. She does not leave the nest. The male crow brings the female crow food as she sits, but he does not sit on the eggs.

Hatching

The eggs hatch after about eighteen days.
The newly hatched chicks are called *hatchlings*.
The female crow helps free the hatchlings from
the eggs with her beak and eats the eggshells.
Both parents clean and fluff the nest around
the babies and make sure they are clean. The
hatchlings are blind and nearly bare of feathers.

Growing

The hatchlings are hungry as soon as they come out of the eggs. The crow parents teach the chicks to open their mouths for food by touching the sides of their beaks. Soon the hatchlings open their eyes, which are blue at first. Older siblings will often come back to help the parents feed and care for the crow chicks.

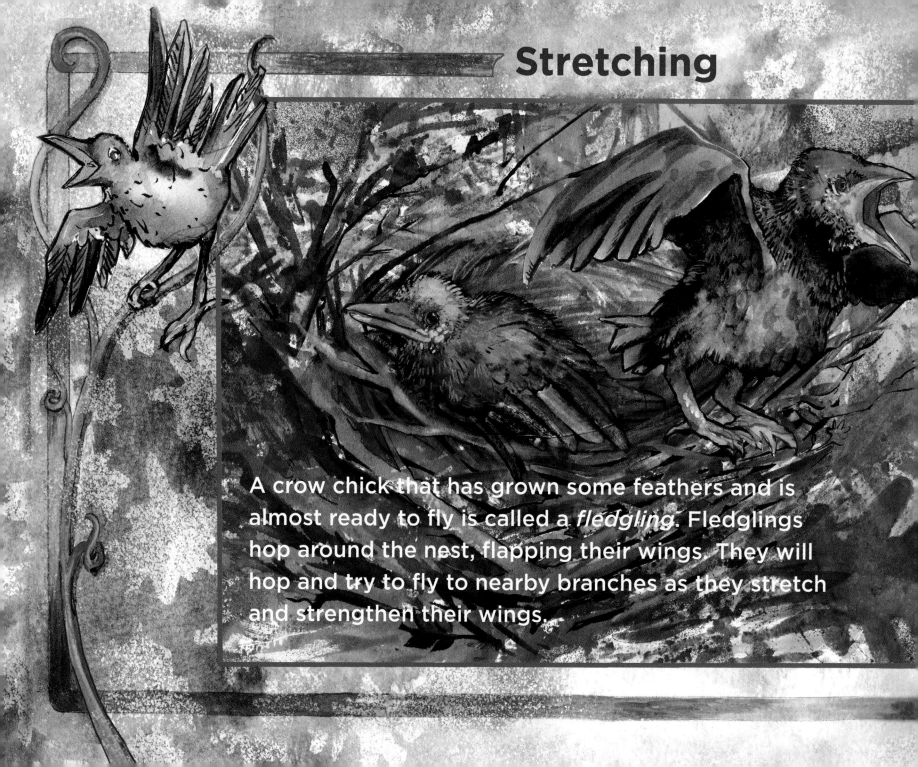

Stretching

A crow chick that has grown some feathers and is almost ready to fly is called a *fledgling*. Fledglings hop around the nest, flapping their wings. They will hop and try to fly to nearby branches as they stretch and strengthen their wings.

Thinking and Playing

Fledglings and adult crows are curious and playful. They are very smart, and this allows them to make and use tools to gather food. Crows also invent games for fun like sledding or dropping and catching a stick in the air. Crows collect and give gifts. Curiosity and wanting to fly can also lead young crows out of the nest before they are quite ready.

Spreading New Wings

A fledgling is ready to fly about thirty to forty days after hatching. Soon they try to fly greater distances, to a branch farther from the nest or to a nearby tree or to a fire escape. Sometimes fledglings end up on the ground.

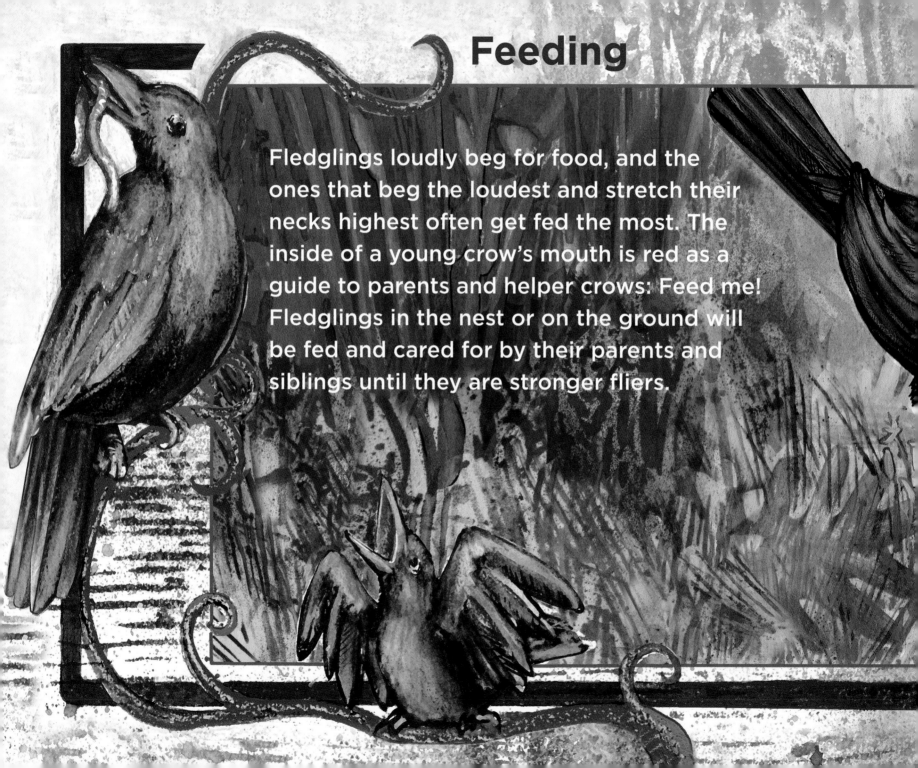

Feeding

Fledglings loudly beg for food, and the ones that beg the loudest and stretch their necks highest often get fed the most. The inside of a young crow's mouth is red as a guide to parents and helper crows: Feed me! Fledglings in the nest or on the ground will be fed and cared for by their parents and siblings until they are stronger fliers.

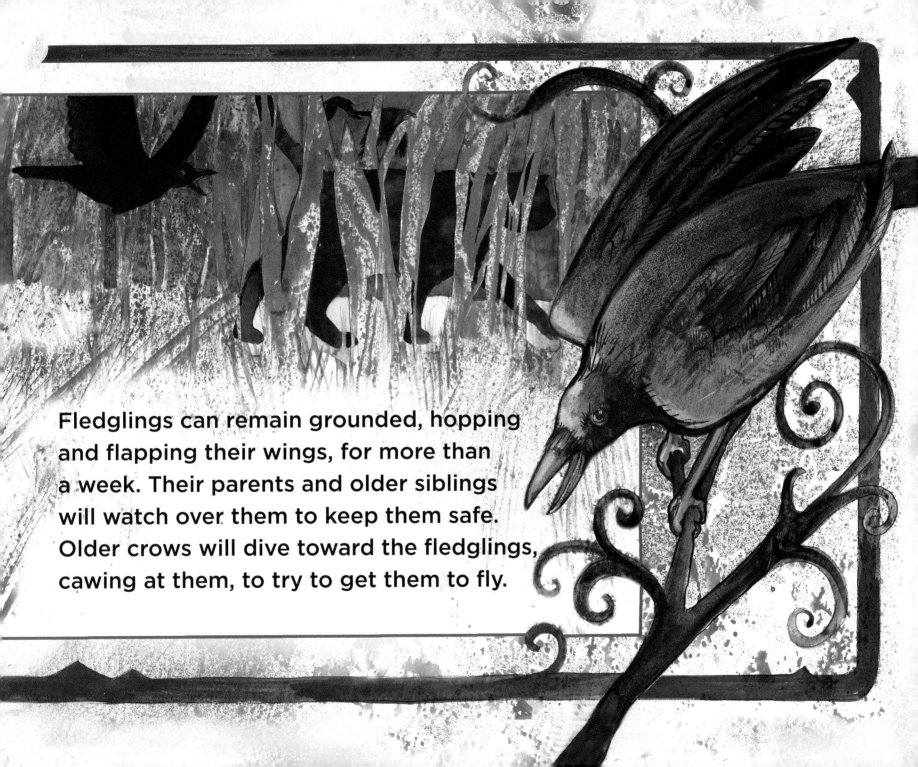

Fledglings can remain grounded, hopping and flapping their wings, for more than a week. Their parents and older siblings will watch over them to keep them safe. Older crows will dive toward the fledglings, cawing at them, to try to get them to fly.

Protecting

Because they are not yet great fliers, fledglings are in danger from predators such as hawks, owls, eagles, cats, and sometimes humans. Crows work together to chase and harass these hunters. This behavior is called *mobbing*. While adult crows distract and mob threats, the fledgling tries to fly.

Trying

Young crows stretch and flap,
hop, and take short flights.

By trying

and trying

and trying

and trying.

. . . and roosting.

Cawing

While crows are roosting, mating, nesting, growing, playing, feeding, protecting, and flying . . . they are cawing.

Crows make lots of sounds, from loud caws to quiet babbling. Scientists do not know exactly what the different sounds mean.

It is hard for humans to tell the difference between crow calls that say "Danger! Watch out!" and crow calls that say "I am here! And I feel great!" and calls that tell other crows where there is a food. This is because these calls just sound loud to us: "Caw! Caw!" or "Ko-ko! Ko-ko!"

When crows are mobbing a threat, they sometimes make a kind of growling sound.

Crow families are known to make noises special to that small family group and not used outside of the family. It is easy to hear gentle care in the soft sounds crows make when taking care of their chicks.

Sometimes crows can be found sitting by themselves, making clicking and rattling sounds, almost like they are talking to themselves.

Comparing Corvids

The American Crow is the second-largest songbird in the United States. The largest is the Common Raven. A raven weighs almost three times as much as a crow, has a heavy curved beak, and fluffy beard-like feathers. A crow is about 17 inches from beak to tail tip, and a raven is about 24 inches long. Crows have a fan-shaped tail, and ravens have a wedge-shaped tail, which makes them easy to tell apart when they are flying.

Ravens spend time alone, and crows spend more time in groups. Crows and ravens both make a lot of different sounds but, basically, crows caw and ravens make a deep croak.

Crows and ravens are part of a larger group of birds scientists call corvids. This group includes rooks, jackdaws, magpies, nutcrackers, and many different kinds of jays.

Corvids are very smart, able to use tools, learn, and play. Their brain power is a lot like gorillas' and chimps'. Corvids can be found on every continent on Earth except Antarctica.

For Sam.

References

Marzluff, John M., and Tony Angell. *In the Company of Crows and Ravens.* Yale University Press, 2005.

Haupt, Lyanda Lynn. *Crow Planet: Essential Wisdom from the Urban Wilderness.* Little Brown, 2009.

Goodwin, Derek. *Crows of the World: An Authoritative Guide to All 116 Species of the Crow Family, Including Jays, Magpies, Rooks, and the Raven.* The Gresham Press, 1976.

Savage, Candace. *Bird Brains: The Intelligence of Crows, Ravens, Magpies, and Jays.* Sierra Club Books, 1995.

An imprint of Globe Pequot, the trade division of
The Rowman & Littlefield Publishing Group, Inc.
4501 Forbes Blvd., Ste. 200
Lanham, MD 20706
www.rowman.com

Distributed by NATIONAL BOOK NETWORK

British Library Cataloguing in Publication Information available

Library of Congress Cataloging-in-Publication Data

Names: Peot, Margaret, author.
Title: Crows : an egg-to-sky story / Margaret Peot.
Description: Essex, Connecticut : Muddy Boots, [2024] | Includes bibliographical references. | Audience: Ages 6-9 | Audience: Grades 2-3
Identifiers: LCCN 2023043826 (print) | LCCN 2023043827 (ebook) | ISBN 9781493080977 (cloth) | ISBN 9781943085804 (epub)
Subjects: LCSH: Crows—Juvenile literature.
Classification: LCC QL696.P2367 P44 2024 (print) | LCC QL696.P2367 (ebook) | DDC 598.8/64—dc23/eng/20231020
LC record available at https://lccn.loc.gov/2023043826
LC ebook record available at https://lccn.loc.gov/2023043827

Printed in India | July 2024